The Solid Proof That Russians Didn't Interfere In Elections

FULL EDITING

By
RICHARD ZORGE

The Solid Proof That Russians Didn't Interfere In Elections

The Solid Proof That Russians Didn't Interfere In Elections

The Solid Proof That Russians Didn't Interfere In Elections

The Solid Proof That Russians Didn't Interfere In Elections

The Solid Proof That Russians Didn't Interfere In Elections

The Solid Proof That Russians Didn't Interfere In Elections

The Solid Proof That Russians Didn't Interfere In Elections

The Solid Proof That Russians Didn't Interfere In Elections

The Solid Proof That Russians Didn't Interfere In Elections

The Solid Proof That Russians Didn't Interfere In Elections

The Solid Proof That Russians Didn't Interfere In Elections

The Solid Proof That Russians Didn't Interfere In Elections

The Solid Proof That Russians Didn't Interfere In Elections

The Solid Proof That Russians Didn't Interfere In Elections

The Solid Proof That Russians Didn't Interfere In Elections

The Solid Proof That Russians Didn't Interfere In Elections

The Solid Proof That Russians Didn't Interfere In Elections

The Solid Proof That Russians Didn't Interfere In Elections

The Solid Proof That Russians Didn't Interfere In Elections

The Solid Proof That Russians Didn't Interfere In Elections

The Solid Proof That Russians Didn't Interfere In Elections

The Solid Proof That Russians Didn't Interfere In Elections

The Solid Proof That Russians Didn't Interfere In Elections

The Solid Proof That Russians Didn't Interfere In Elections

The Solid Proof That Russians Didn't Interfere In Elections

The Solid Proof That Russians Didn't Interfere In Elections

The Solid Proof That Russians Didn't Interfere In Elections

The Solid Proof That Russians Didn't
Interfere In Elections

The Solid Proof That Russians Didn't Interfere In Elections

The Solid Proof That Russians Didn't Interfere In Elections

The Solid Proof That Russians Didn't Interfere In Elections

The Solid Proof That Russians Didn't Interfere In Elections

The Solid Proof That Russians Didn't Interfere In Elections

The Solid Proof That Russians Didn't Interfere In Elections

The Solid Proof That Russians Didn't Interfere In Elections

The Solid Proof That Russians Didn't Interfere In Elections

The Solid Proof That Russians Didn't Interfere In Elections

The Solid Proof That Russians Didn't
Interfere In Elections

The Solid Proof That Russians Didn't Interfere In Elections

The Solid Proof That Russians Didn't Interfere In Elections

The Solid Proof That Russians Didn't Interfere In Elections

The Solid Proof That Russians Didn't Interfere In Elections

The Solid Proof That Russians Didn't Interfere In Elections

The Solid Proof That Russians Didn't Interfere In Elections

The Solid Proof That Russians Didn't Interfere In Elections

The Solid Proof That Russians Didn't Interfere In Elections

The Solid Proof That Russians Didn't Interfere In Elections

The Solid Proof That Russians Didn't Interfere In Elections

The Solid Proof That Russians Didn't Interfere In Elections

The Solid Proof That Russians Didn't Interfere In Elections

The Solid Proof That Russians Didn't Interfere In Elections

The Solid Proof That Russians Didn't Interfere In Elections

The Solid Proof That Russians Didn't Interfere In Elections

The Solid Proof That Russians Didn't Interfere In Elections

The Solid Proof That Russians Didn't Interfere In Elections

The Solid Proof That Russians Didn't Interfere In Elections

The Solid Proof That Russians Didn't Interfere In Elections

The Solid Proof That Russians Didn't Interfere In Elections

The Solid Proof That Russians Didn't Interfere In Elections

The Solid Proof That Russians Didn't
Interfere In Elections

The Solid Proof That Russians Didn't
Interfere In Elections

The Solid Proof That Russians Didn't Interfere In Elections

The Solid Proof That Russians Didn't Interfere In Elections

The Solid Proof That Russians Didn't Interfere In Elections

The Solid Proof That Russians Didn't Interfere In Elections

The Solid Proof That Russians Didn't Interfere In Elections

The Solid Proof That Russians Didn't Interfere In Elections

The Solid Proof That Russians Didn't Interfere In Elections

The Solid Proof That Russians Didn't Interfere In Elections

The Solid Proof That Russians Didn't Interfere In Elections

The Solid Proof That Russians Didn't Interfere In Elections

The Solid Proof That Russians Didn't Interfere In Elections

The Solid Proof That Russians Didn't Interfere In Elections

The Solid Proof That Russians Didn't Interfere In Elections

The Solid Proof That Russians Didn't Interfere In Elections

The Solid Proof That Russians Didn't Interfere In Elections

The Solid Proof That Russians Didn't Interfere In Elections

The Solid Proof That Russians Didn't Interfere In Elections

The Solid Proof That Russians Didn't Interfere In Elections

The Solid Proof That Russians Didn't Interfere In Elections

The Solid Proof That Russians Didn't Interfere In Elections

The Solid Proof That Russians Didn't Interfere In Elections

The Solid Proof That Russians Didn't Interfere In Elections

The Solid Proof That Russians Didn't Interfere In Elections

The Solid Proof That Russians Didn't Interfere In Elections

The Solid Proof That Russians Didn't Interfere In Elections

The Solid Proof That Russians Didn't Interfere In Elections

The Solid Proof That Russians Didn't Interfere In Elections

The Solid Proof That Russians Didn't Interfere In Elections

The Solid Proof That Russians Didn't Interfere In Elections

The Solid Proof That Russians Didn't Interfere In Elections

The Solid Proof That Russians Didn't Interfere In Elections

The Solid Proof That Russians Didn't Interfere In Elections

The Solid Proof That Russians Didn't Interfere In Elections

The Solid Proof That Russians Didn't Interfere In Elections

The Solid Proof That Russians Didn't Interfere In Elections

The Solid Proof That Russians Didn't Interfere In Elections

The Solid Proof That Russians Didn't Interfere In Elections

The Solid Proof That Russians Didn't Interfere In Elections

The Solid Proof That Russians Didn't Interfere In Elections

The Solid Proof That Russians Didn't Interfere In Elections

The Solid Proof That Russians Didn't Interfere In Elections

The Solid Proof That Russians Didn't Interfere In Elections

The Solid Proof That Russians Didn't Interfere In Elections

The Solid Proof That Russians Didn't Interfere In Elections

The Solid Proof That Russians Didn't
Interfere In Elections

The Solid Proof That Russians Didn't Interfere In Elections

The Solid Proof That Russians Didn't Interfere In Elections

The Solid Proof That Russians Didn't Interfere In Elections

The Solid Proof That Russians Didn't Interfere In Elections

The Solid Proof That Russians Didn't Interfere In Elections

The Solid Proof That Russians Didn't Interfere In Elections

The Solid Proof That Russians Didn't Interfere In Elections

The Solid Proof That Russians Didn't Interfere In Elections

The Solid Proof That Russians Didn't Interfere In Elections

The Solid Proof That Russians Didn't Interfere In Elections

The Solid Proof That Russians Didn't Interfere In Elections

The Solid Proof That Russians Didn't Interfere In Elections

The Solid Proof That Russians Didn't Interfere In Elections

The Solid Proof That Russians Didn't Interfere In Elections

The Solid Proof That Russians Didn't Interfere In Elections

The Solid Proof That Russians Didn't Interfere In Elections

The Solid Proof That Russians Didn't Interfere In Elections

The Solid Proof That Russians Didn't Interfere In Elections

The Solid Proof That Russians Didn't Interfere In Elections

The Solid Proof That Russians Didn't Interfere In Elections

The Solid Proof That Russians Didn't Interfere In Elections

The Solid Proof That Russians Didn't Interfere In Elections

The Solid Proof That Russians Didn't Interfere In Elections

The Solid Proof That Russians Didn't Interfere In Elections

The Solid Proof That Russians Didn't Interfere In Elections

The Solid Proof That Russians Didn't Interfere In Elections

The Solid Proof That Russians Didn't Interfere In Elections

The Solid Proof That Russians Didn't Interfere In Elections

The Solid Proof That Russians Didn't Interfere In Elections

The Solid Proof That Russians Didn't Interfere In Elections

The Solid Proof That Russians Didn't Interfere In Elections

The Solid Proof That Russians Didn't Interfere In Elections

The Solid Proof That Russians Didn't Interfere In Elections

The Solid Proof That Russians Didn't Interfere In Elections

The Solid Proof That Russians Didn't Interfere In Elections

The Solid Proof That Russians Didn't Interfere In Elections

The Solid Proof That Russians Didn't Interfere In Elections

The Solid Proof That Russians Didn't Interfere In Elections